Tales of an Anxious Hiker

poems by

Heather Kolf

Finishing Line Press
Georgetown, Kentucky

Tales of an Anxious Hiker

ACKNOWLEDGMENTS

"Grief is Expensive" and "Prelude" previously published in
The Banyan Review

"January" and "Yes, You Need Bug Spray" previously
published in *Peninsula Poets*

Publisher: Leah Huete de Maines
Editor: Christen Kincaid
Cover Art: Heather Kolf
Author Photo: Mary Pencheff Photography
Cover Design: Elizabeth Maines McCleavy

Order online: www.finishinglinepress.com
also available on amazon.com

Author inquiries and mail orders:
Finishing Line Press
PO Box 1626
Georgetown, Kentucky 40324
USA

Contents

Prelude

one of my favorite ways to see the forest
is in the upside down reflection of tree tops in a still pond
or a swamp
I'm not picky

this trick is so marvelous to me
look! it's nature
showing you nature
we like to think ours is the only perspective
but nature writes poems about itself in the water
and in the sky
all the stories of your life are written on the trail
and on the river
and everything you could ever know is in the dirt
and the leaves of trees

The Weather and The Writing

It comes in fits and starts today
a single line that goes nowhere
a thought too big for the page
Like my hike today
walking the same icy path
back and forth between hills
repeatedly starting over
and repeatedly going nowhere
I stayed where I felt safe
I was after all alone in the woods
and constantly calculating how
far I would have to crawl
in the snow back to my car
if I sprained an ankle
I am nothing if not vigilant
For all my preparation
I am not prepared
I put the snow spikes in the car
and forgot to put them on
This is how I do things
Plan for days weeks months
even years and then
forget
a houseful of weatherproof clothes
and me standing naked in a blizzard

Oh Christmas Tree

It starts as a joke among friends
drunken thirty-something shenanigans
or maybe a family of four plus dog
or a lone hiker
carrying bulbs of silver or red or memory
in wine boxes or plastic bags or sweater pockets
out to the middle of the forest

Pick a tree
Any tree

The tipsy gang near midnight choose three right at the trailhead
throwing ornaments on only one side of the first pines they see
as if to say "Welcome" and "This sounded better back at the bar"
The family purposeful and unhurried spend the morning
searching for a perfectly sparse Charlie Brown tree
branches bowing under the weight of
five ornaments tap dancing on top of the crusted snow
Those in search of winter quiet
carry their gifts in pockets
hidden, inconspicuous
they venture deepest into the woods
aiming to connect and say "I was here too"

And then there are the golden few who
saddled with loss and sadness and the holidays
make their own decorations to hang
black marker on wood cutout rings
Keep Going exclamation point with a smiley face
You're Doing Great exclamation point with stars
and my favorite

Keep Shining Bright

just
that

when I
saddled with loss and sadness and the holidays
didn't think I was

January

They say
the sun always rises

They

have never seen a Michigan winter

Grief is Expensive

I think I might be
buying a coffee table
in order to
avoid certain feelings

what used to be ice cream
has become
furniture
I'm sure it's a sign I'm maturing

I know the feelings are coming
in quiet moments
I sense the rumble beneath my
feet the fire at my back
the fifty foot wave above me
which is paused for now

in mid air

while I
place an order on Etsy
for a handmade herringbone coffee table

in toasted walnut

Lake Michigan

Sometimes you just have to go make sure Lake Michigan is still there
you know?
Doesn't matter that the calendar says January
or that the drive from Detroit will be snowswept
The Lake beckons
you just have to go

Lucky for you a layer of snow paints the sandy trail
soft white against muted gray skies
You say hello to a man as you pass
he says nothing and stares at the ground
Clearly he's a murderer

So many animal prints
deer rabbits foxes dogs
Those are dog prints, right?
But what do cougar prints look like in the snow?

You follow the red arrows spray-painted on the trees
(you will consider how you feel about this trail marking schema later)
some are confusing pointing in a direction with no trail
some look like the number five with an arrow on top
one points straight up to the sky
You follow this trail with your eyes and see that it does indeed
go straight up a seven hundred foot sand dune and touch the sky

You take a breath and begin
Climb one step forward slide two steps back
Yeah, no

Searching for another way you end up
in the Valley of the Dunes
From here you can hear Lake Michigan
ferocious and unforgiving
just beyond the sand mountain in front of you
you haven't seen a person since The Killer

it's quiet here
just waves crashing on a shore you can't see

Fewer boot prints mark the path until there are no more
You stand still before undisturbed snow
Do you go forward?

You haven't seen the lake yet part of your brain says
Remember you are alone in the woods and it is twenty eight degrees
and there is likely a killer on the loose not to mention a cougar
the other part argues

you turn back
defeated
without
a glimpse of
Lake Michigan

How would it have felt to take one more step?
the thought whispers itself to you

To be the only footprints in new snow?

Almost to the parking lot now you spot a turn off you didn't take
a steep hike up
I have to try

one step forward
slide half a step back
one step forward
until you arrive
at a man at the top
"Oh" you say
"I'm sorry, I wasn't expecting anyone" and you smile

he wears a black expedition coat carries a serious camera
and looks at you with an expression that says
something smells rotten here
he says nothing
Ah, so HE's the killer

as you calculate how fast you can escape in the snow and sand
you see a small figure in the distance coming your way
a young boy running up the dune you want to warn him
No no no go back the other way!
The boy yells in German and the man
yells back
in German

Oh

Your heart slows
you finally look around
winding paths through snow-covered dunes
and in the distance beneath a dramatic Winter sky
You see for the first time

Lake Michigan

What joy!
What luck!
You take thirty two pictures of the same scene and
wait for the Germans to leave

The trek back to the car is a flurry of people
a couple holding hands a family with sleds a woman and her
dog
The trail feels friendly and inviting now
as if 2pm were the welcoming hour
as if the sun might actually crack through the clouds

but no
this is Michigan
and it's still January

Untitled #1

loud snow under foot
nothing but brown trees black geese
and a memory

Mid Winter Thaw at the Park

Moody unsnowing sky and
a sidewalk lined with dirty snow
they're predicting sleet today
half-melted snowmen
in the distance
kids bounce a basketball in a puddle to see who can make the biggest
splash
bundled up parents push bundled up kids on the swings
voices fade as I enter the woods

I expected mud and I am not disappointed
patches of snow in the wheat-colored tall grass like dollops of
whipped cream I think of hot chocolate and search my memory to
see if I have all of the ingredients
the river awake and mumbling

I try to listen to my thoughts
I've been avoiding them for days
not the planning doing distraction
but the real thoughts
a new job
how did I get here
and this is not who I am supposed to be

Of all the states of being
I like transition the least
the sleet of existence
not quite one thing
not quite another
leaving me half-melted and frozen
I don't do well in the in between
does anyone

kids throw coats in a pile and chase after a
basketball now made soccer ball
a girl in a hat with a brilliant red pompom darts
back to the coat hill
finds her matching red jacket
puts it on
and runs to catch up

A Friendly Hiking Challenge Between Sisters

She hikes in California
each picture a golden mountain rainbow ocean treasure
I hike in the Michigan winter
each picture desperately trying to make gray trees look
interesting
it's not a competition we both say
but what number hike are you on?

We struggle with motivation
injuries
life
but we persevere
often only because the other one is
persevering
but that is
inspiration
we say
not competition

We each hike more and further
because of the other
seeking out new trails
finding old favorites
and discovering what we're made of
reluctant grit
slothful determination
and a complete
lack
of competitiveness

When the time comes
I imagine our conversation

I finished the challenge first
I say

And she of course doesn't miss a beat

Ah but who had more fun?

The Last Day of the World

On the last day of the world, I would want to plant a tree.
—W.S. Merwin

On the last day of the world, I would also want to plant a tree
And watch the sun
rise
And write a poem
And read a poem
And walk in the woods
And spend time with the people I love
And eat cake and tacos and Greek salad and French fries fried in
good old fashioned trans fat
And run around furiously trying to fix this
last day of the world problem
then come to the end of it
watch the sun
set
and find peace

a radical acceptance
maybe around a campfire
with marshmallows
and family and friends
where we would try to say meaningful things
and we would fail

on the last day of the world
I would be glad I planted a tree

and also that I ate tacos

Invisible Threads

I'm watching a leaf dance in a humid breeze
but she doesn't fall to the ground this one
she seems to twirl in place and keep a rhythm
all her own I come closer and see she is

suspended

in a spider's web
halfway
between

branch

and

ground

she seems to be stuck there
but making the best of it

the green pixie dazzles in her show
audience or not
and the sun sets her aglow as she spins

invisible threads dangle her
out into the middle of the path
giving the illusion she is
somehow defying
gravity

and I am reminded once again

nature
is the original
magic

Yes, You Need Bug Spray

I'm in it for the pizza this hike
this muggy buggy boggy hike
as the mosquitoes swarm I remember the bug spray
I left in the car
I have no armor against the invading forces
and I am unshowered
I will undoubtedly be eaten alive smelly as I am

which makes me think of Jeff Daniels

not because he's smelly
no
because I am hiking in his hometown
and I wonder if I'll run into him on the trail
my gritty, grimy, bitten-up self the humidity wrapping me in an
invisible film that only slows me down and suffocates like I'm
pushing forward through a giant outstretched saran wrap that
still allows the bugs in of course
the sweat would drip I'm sure were it wetter than the air
but no

instead sweat sits on my skin and seeps into my hair and when I
run the back of my hand across the top of my forehead I only
succeed in smoothing out the drops into a fine glisten
I am coated in bodily fluids, dead bugs and swamp air
I am gross
I am miserable
I am certain I will run into Jeff Daniels today

Heading back to the car dreaming of deep dish and a shower I
wondered if
my misery and pushing through had made me any
stronger
or if the fact that I was miserable at all
showed a weakness

or something else altogether
and I kind of wished my
wondering wandering questioning self
had
run into Jeff Daniels
because I've never met him but he seems like someone who might
want to talk about these kinds of things for a minute

or at least until he smelled me

Like Wind Chill

Heading south to Ohio to beat the heat was not the
best idea I've had this summer

I blame the heat

it's too hot to think things through or care really
a searing apathy
a blistering indifference
a scorching unconcern envelops
this Pandemic Second Summer
this Summer
for the Mosquito
of the Mosquito
and by the Mosquito this
Suffocating Summer on Fire

At a critical junction
I spy a hula hoop
hung around a trail sign
As if to say
this is where joy has come to die

I picture the scene
A seven year old girl hangs the hoop to
tie her shoes
the whining comes later
But Mom
I lost my hula hoop
I wanna go home
and I realize I've said that last line out loud

on another day in another year
I a forty seven year old woman with graying hair
might have hula hooped my way back to the car
but this so-called loop trail
has gone on for at least eleven straight miles
(my step counter reads three point one

but we all know those things are horribly inaccurate)
plus I'm factoring in the humidity
which is like wind chill
only worse

Go Play Outside

A blue jay screaming in the distance on the trail today
somehow whispers to me scenes from a cottage kitchen
St. Helen Michigan 1981
I can smell the bacon and the humidity
go play outside
someone always seemed to be saying
but not in the sleepy mornings
when Grandma still in her curlers and pink housecoat
lets me sit on her lap and sip her coffee
mom to my right
dad leaning on the counter
more people than chairs in the mornings
all of us crowded into that ten by ten room
I loved that kitchen
I felt safe in that kitchen
later when someone tells me to
think of a happy time
I think of this

after breakfast we mom and all the girls would go for a walk
down the dirt road out past the marina
picking wildflowers and learning the names of things
which is where I
distracted and half listening and seven years old
came to believe that bumblebees were called yellowjackets
because it made perfect sense that a bee with a furry coat
would have jacket in its name

later at the beach I would dive deep
and come up with a sliver of driftwood buried in my skin
requiring a trip to the IGA for tweezers and a stuffed pig I named
Penelope
the adults took turns working that splinter
and I wailed the whole time clutching Penelope to my heart
but the instant it came free I was back chasing
chipmunks in the sandbox that was our whole yard

the jay cries again and now I'm back at the Whitney Portal Store
eating a BLT on the patio and playing Scrabble in the shade
Mt. Whitney 2005
with my Aunt Theo and Uncle Dave
tomorrow we will start up the mountain
tomorrow
my stomach does loops with every thought of it
the heat the hike the haul
packs weighing in at 42 pounds each
how many water filters do we really need?
I focus on my letters and the bacon
and for a second I capture this memory with all of my senses

the jay hollers again and I'm back on the trail
bored and heavy in the thick heat of a Michigan summer
suffocating and free at the same time
no wonder I was so easily taken with the past

I don't always notice the miracle in nature
see the gift in every tree
sometimes I just see a jumbled mess of green and brown
and wonder what the big deal is
that's just the truth
sometimes the forest is a giant screen for me to
play home movies on
sometimes the trail is the face of a jerk I'd like to stomp and
sometimes the sky is the canvas for my
depression

I guess what I'm saying is that
sometimes I miss the point of getting out in nature
and sometimes
that is the point
of getting out in nature

Untitled #2

worms worms and more worms
storm blew through this afternoon
where is the late bird

The Dead Thing

Today in the woods there is a ringing and it calls to me
a high pitched hum
natural
and unnatural
at the same time
I seem to be moving closer until I realize I am
moving further away
somewhere in there is the center
but of what

I move into a meadow and a
lone hawk coasts in a circle above me
a black silhouette against white sky
I hear a helicopter I can't see
while frantic birds screech and flap to warn me
but of what

Something died
I'm sure of it

It's about this time in the hike when I think
Maybe I shouldn't have watched that
Steven King interview before
heading out on the trail today

I'm sure there's a perfectly rational explanation for all of this

But I come to the edge of the woods
and the one note song beckons me
I feel powerless and pulled
The hawk draws closer
My step forward feels
automatic
and outside of myself
The helicopter apocalyptic now
Birds flail and fall and call and cry

and in the middle of it all
the hum wraps itself around me
I feel comforted

and then I think

what if I am the dead thing

Dear Seventy Percent Humidity

I'm sorry to say
you serve no purpose
in the weather food chain.
If anything
you're a sign of a flaw in our clouds
allowing water to leak into the air like that.

This sounds like an engineering problem.
Can't we fix that
with some duct tape
or Tyvek?

Of course I know that's not how it works,
but I'd like to enjoy a Michigan summer for once
and not be swallowed up, coughed out
and trapped in the phlegm of one.

I mean,
don't you have a passion?
Something else you'd enjoy?
Or do you just enjoy
the misery of others
like mosquitoes
and those people who steal identities?
Surely if you took one of those
career assessments
there would be something else out there for you.
Mine always suggested
clergy
but maybe you'll have better luck.

Yes, I know, we welcome your cousin,
Thirty Percent Humidity,
and I imagine that hurts.
It's not that we don't accept you for who you are.
We do.

We just think maybe you'd be better suited to
another line of work.

Anyway, I've got to get going here.
But think about it.
And let's talk next week.
My schedule is free until Thursday
when I have a phone call with the mosquitoes
at two o'clock.

Big Orange Quiet

I do most of my
best thinking
and most of my best
not thinking
while watching the
sun set

A Thousand Words

Sometimes
the best thing I see on a hike
is my car in the parking lot as I near the end
that's just the truth

what a beautiful forest
you would say
looking at the photos
but humidity hates to have its picture taken
as does the urgent itch of a mosquito bite
and the chemical smell of green algae on a still pond

on those days
the forest is like a dysfunctional family
with someone saying
but we always looked so happy in the pictures

Well, Hello There

There are turkeys on the trail
Apparently it's their trail I had no idea
They herd me off to the side like I'm a sheep
They know me so well

The place is lousy with woodpeckers
red-headed something or other
I love nature but not in the way that I can identify everything
I guess it's more of a feeling-kind-of-love than a naming-kind-of-love

A chipmunk scolds me for being too close to the entrance of his
home I say I'm sorry and he disappears into the darkness
his tail lingering for a minute as if to say
here's what I think of your apology

Snakes only seem to appear when I'm with other people
which is just fine with me I'm not afraid or anything
and company seems to be
the best method for keeping it that way

I'm skittish walking through spider webs
especially the ones that are face high
or finding moth larva on my shoulder or worse
in my hair or later in a pocket
But I startle the most when other people on the trail don't say hello
Sure they could just be distracted or deep in thought I suppose

like quiet little serial killers

deep in murderous thought

After the Flood

So it's a gross hike
swampy after days of downpours that
inspired jet ski rides at city intersections
flies with speckled wings land on the lenses of my glasses
the air so thick with mosquitoes I inhale them by the dozens
a protein snack I suppose if I'm bright-siding it
But I'm not
I'm in a mood today
Grief will do that to you

I don't know if I believe in closure exactly
but waiting for funerals in the pandemic has definitely
left something open

today I misread a sign on the trail and ended up at R2
Yeah, I don't know where that is either
I was expecting Y6
and when I realized I'd added another mile to this pathetic
excuse for a day spent in nature
I cried
I didn't fall on the wet ground or anything
but angry tears streamed down my cheeks
and wiping them away, I also rid the planet of one mosquito
one who took advantage of my vulnerable state
one less jerk mosquito
you're welcome

I round the bend to the sound of a baby bird crying for its mother
or at least that's what I imagine
why else do baby birds cry?
certainly not because they've added a measly mile to their
journey

the crying bird means I'm close to the car
I step into a clearing and notice
translucent orange berries glowing in the sunlight
I've never seen orange berries like this before

they could be teenage red berries I suppose
or more likely just another thing I've never noticed

but for now
for today
I choose to believe
I need to believe
orange berries are magic
and a sign of good things to come

orange berries are forged in the
unforgiving mud of this path

and orange berries always
and only
appear
after the flood

Tucson Arizona October 2021

Sunshine and solace
Finally
Mom and I take to the trail together in the morning
After tough nights in the desert

A wandering path in Saguaro National Park
The sun is different here
Powerful and restorative
We are easy with one another now
Laughing and smiling and knowing
This is her brother's country
A country of memory and beauty and dust

We climb out of the dry wash to an overlook
All of Tucson laid out below us
We take our picture
The sun warm and loving

Weeks later I scratch the spot where
a cholla spine lodged itself in my calf that day
An image of mom in her hiking hat flashes in my mind
And even the sting of a defensive cactus feels sweet to me now

Hard Things

On the trail today
I listen to the first verse of American Pie
a song my dad would play on the accordion
yes the accordion
he died a year ago tomorrow
but it's an older grief

The song chose itself at random
so I know my dad is trying to tell me something
and when I listen I hear
music wasn't just something he loved
music
was how he loved us

this trick is so marvelous to me
how time passing and some song lyrics can conjure real feeling
real love
and how the reflection can be clearer
than the hurt

I come to the woods with hard things
things that keep me distracted
and sometimes I forget
sometimes I'm so wrapped up in a song
or a memory
that I miss the duck or the turtle
but today
after the rain painted the dirt almost black
and the leaves shiny pink and gold
today
the forest reminds me

I can both
miss everything
and see it all in reflection

at the same time

With Thanks

I have so many people to thank for all of the different roles they played in the writing of this collection. First, I'd like to thank my mom for being my biggest cheerleader from the start. I couldn't have done this without your unwavering love and support.

Most of these poems were written during a year-long (okay, 59 weeks, but who's counting) hiking challenge that I did with my sister, Becky—hey Becky, we made it! And, also, I won. But seriously, thanks for all the inspiration.

My sister, Kelly, was instrumental in helping out with things waaay outside of my comfort zone. (Author photos are no joke!) Thank you!

And to my Aunt Theo, thank you so much for your excellent feedback and loving support—always.

I'd like to thank the Writers' Colony at Dairy Hollow, whose residency was not only life-changing, but also the key to my finishing this collection.

And, of course, to Dawn and the Usual Suspects at my Sunday afternoon Shut Up and Write group—this wouldn't even exist if it weren't for you guys—you're the best!

To poets Robin Carstensen, Bonnie Bishop and Matthew Olzmann, thank you all so much for your time and thoughtful words.

To Mary Pencheff, thank you for your wonderful photos.

And to everyone at Finishing Line Press—thank you for your role in making this dream come true.

Finally, to all of my family and friends who inspired, encouraged and stood by me throughout this process (you know who you are!), from my whole heart,
thank you.

Heather Kolf holds a Master of Arts in English from Wayne State University in Detroit where she focused on both creative writing and literature. Her poems have appeared in The Banyan Review as well as Peninsula Poets. Tales of an Anxious Hiker is her first poetry collection.

She is also a recovering baseball blogger (under a pen name), and her past projects include a screenplay collaboration for the independent film *Detroit Unleaded*, which premiered at the Toronto International Film Festival. Weekdays, she works as an Oncology Data Specialist, abstracting data for cancer research. On the weekends, she often wanders around in the Michigan woods.

Sometimes lost.

Sometimes found.